ANIMATED LANDSCAPE

ANIMATED LANDSCAPE

ROBERT GIBBONS

BLAZEVOX[BOOKS]
Buffalo, New York

First Edition
ISBN: 978-1-60964-257-0
Library of Congress Control Number: 2016937145

BlazeVOX [books]
131 Euclid Ave
Kenmore, NY 14217
Editor@blazevox.org

publisher of weird little books

BlazeVOX [books]

blazevox.org

21 20 19 18 17 16 15 14 13 12 01 02 03 04 05 06 07 08 09 10

BlazeVOX

Contents

With the exception of most Native Americans and a few non-natives who have given their hearts to the place, the land we all live on is simply taken for granted – and proper relation to it is not considered part of 'citizenship.' But after two centuries of national history, people are beginning to wake up and notice that the Unites States is located on a landscape with a severe, spectacular, spacy, wildly demanding, and ecstatic narrative to be learned.

—Gary Snyder, *Coming into the Watershed*

The archetype here is the *participation mystique* of primitive man with the soil on which he dwells, and which contains the spirits of his ancestors... The journey through the psychic history of mankind has as its object the restoration of the whole man/[woman], by awakening the memories in the blood.

—C. G. Jung, *The Spirit in Man, Art, and Literature*

He has space and then damnwell goes on and acts-as surely he has, terrifically, for 50,000 years (those paintings, there, Altamira, and his feet in the dirt before those paintings still showing, until right... this minute...

—Charles Olson, *Letter to Robert Creeley, May 15, 1952*

> *But having had a light from an ember*
> *and standing there, I marveled at the beauty*
> *of men with long hair.   Yes, it is quite*
> *different.   Their world.   I am sure they tread*
> *upon an Earth I don't. And I would like to.*

—Edward Dorn, *"The Land Below"*

Memory is the medium of what has been experienced the way the earthen realm is the medium in which dead cities lie buried. He who wishes to approach his own buried past must act like a man who digs.

—Walter Benjamin, *Berlin Chronicle*

for Kathleen, who knows the motives
& the meanings

ANIMATED LANDSCAPE

They Drew That Perfect Bird

The exact technique of how they drew that perfect
bird out of stone is lost. But not the desire to
render fauna & flora we see, those osprey,
even the gull, if need be, & this native
hobblebush. If one can't accomplish
it in stone, or paint, jot down color
& shape, curve of wing, angle
of beak. Calyx, leaf, & petal.
Speed of flight & scent of
flower in the wind.

First I've Heard

Delightfully diligent bordering
on relentless, the cardinal this spring
must have found a home near here, & sings
for a mate. It's Joyful, really, & constant reminder
of all possible audible Joys. I muted the classical station
playing Telemann in order to catch the first I've heard this
year of the woodpecker. It reminded me of the guy on Saturday
staring intensely up into a stand of birches to attempt to identify
the source of what he heard. The freshness of his seeing bordered
on the aboriginal.

Weaving, Dancing, Spinning

My woman's out by the fire weaving
texts. In the dream a soldier asked
her to dance, responding only if
I gave consent. I gave consent,
if she saved the last for me.
The Huichols use woven
yarn & beeswax in order
to make *nearikas*: faces,
aspects, designs on
sacred stones.

Woman out by the fire spinning yarn
for *nearikas*, texts. I gave consent
in the dream to the soldier, who
danced on. Raptor's claw, bison
horn, bear paw, the Huichols
call up spirit faces, aspects,
designs on sacred stones.
Yarn color: yellow, red.
Soldier's uniform blue.

Joys of the Incidental

That's just it, too: Joys
of the incidental, as well
as depths of perception: what
with Roy Hargrove in the background
live at the New Morning in Paris on *Strasbourg –*
St. Denis, the cardinal out the open window chiming
in, & Zbigniew Herbert down there in Lascaux comparing
the subtleties of the animals drawn on the walls to the warmth
& tenderness of Modigliani's Women, & the passion invested in
the Black Bulls echoing in Goya.

At the Speed of Light

There's a brand new beam of light,
strong enough to be a rafter if strung across
the ceiling, strafing corner bookcase Kline, Rothko,
Pollock, de Kooning, Kapoor catalogues on the top shelf
just above photographers Francesca Woodman, Man Ray,
Brassaï (with whom I was in the same room), Robert Frank,
& Rauschenberg (with whom I was also present), gathering together
their share of moments perpetuated at the speed of light right up to this
February 18th morning with Charles Lloyd wafting on tenor & flute over
airwaves out of San Francisco at 4:16 a.m. their time on *Forest Flower Sunrise*
with Keith Jarrett piano, Cecil McBee bass, Jack DeJohnette drums
coffee on she's upstairs practicing yoga sun repositioning itself
casting new ray of light my way in the kitchen touching
current one with skin still riding that earlier
shaft of light strafing corner bookcase
Kline, Rothko, Pollock, de Kooning,
Kapoor wondering where that not
so ephemeral energy
went?

Exact Geographical Match

If the sun
seems blindingly
bright, against white
clapboards on the shed
in the backyard, blame it
on the previous three days near
misery: dark, stuck low pressure,
remnant of some system took parts
of Texas along with it. This lone star
may still lead me down where I chose
not to go, but will seek out, believe me,
that path through birches, thorns, jagged
stones, the clearing I know so well the back
of my hand is all a renewed sun will need take
to help me find that exact geographical match
with land & sea of my own rejuvenated solitude.

Secret & Terrible Places

Gave the dream class a simple assignment: Read these
books. Books from my own library: Apollinaire,
Barthes, Baudelaire, Camus, (wasn't it
Mandelstam who said don't tell me
about the lives of writers, just list
the books they read?) Cavafy,
Cixous, Dostoevsky, Elytis,
etc.

Every desk occupied, they were silent, reading,
until I glanced at the clock, (the famous
clock on the classroom wall), when
I said, "Alright, exchange books."

Then, & only then, a voice
from the back of the room,
"Are these inspiration
for your writing?"

"No, they are validation for it.
Writing comes from the heart
& stomach, secret & terrible
places (I pictured them
there in this dream,
having had X-rays
the day before),
which I value."

Will to Freedom

If the sea hates one thing, it's the seawall.
In the middle of the night I heard it
growl & roar like a pride
of angry lions.
Hungry for stones.
This morning, evidence strewn all over
the place, the battered wall
in need of repair.
At various points
along the shore there are gaps
& spaces where no houses could ever stand,
entire stretches where the sea challenges
land for ownership.
"Want that marshland," chant the waves.
It's a constant threat of invasion,
or reclaiming what it lost
to so-called civilization.
In its will to freedom
the sea hates
one thing,
the seawall.

Uncoiling Scroll of Brutal Force

There's a charging
Bison on the ceiling
of Altamira exemplifies
the compulsion Olson saw
as the origin of any language
act. The word *volute* just came
to me out of some undisclosed well
within = bison is rolled into dynamic
ball uncoiling scroll of brutal force, horned
weapon, testeronic origin of energy, not syntax,
as Charles points out, but below & behind, at origin.
If generation is the feminine counterpart outlined by
docile hind, or perfected in the molded vulva at *Bédeilhac,*
this masculine prototype is just why the poet goes so rapidly
toward the dramatic stage of Aeschylus & Homer's blind chant
of War.

Spain's *Red Lady*

They named her Spain's *Red Lady*.

Discovered in El Mirón Cave in 2010,
she was between thirty-five & forty-years-old
at the time of her death during the Magdalenian.

A hundred bones painted with ochre.

Recently, archaeologists found pollen
samples among the remains,
suggesting she was buried
ceremoniously with flowers
from the goosefoot family.

They also speculate that her corpse
was left to decompose before
painting her spirit
with the iron-oxide.

She was healthy,
living on a diet
of deer, fish,
& fungi.

The limestone marker
covering Spain's *Red Lady*,
which fell from the ceiling,
has a series of V-shapes
etched in the stone.

There's a sense
of somber beauty,
& ongoing mourning
to the whole story.

An Aesthetic Dilemma

Magdalenian painters struggled with the conflict
that their prey was the subject of their art.
Max Raphael called it an aesthetic
dilemma. He speculates that one
solution remained: Beauty.

The French philosopher offers the hind at Altamira
as the prime example. The subtlety draws back
away from reality, transposing an ideal view.
What strikes me here is that he sees the line
of ideal Beauty in art flow eighteen
millennia down to modern Paris,
where he suggests the mold
was broken by of all artists,
a poet: Charles Baudelaire.

Sandstone Lamp

Out here in the shack, sources
piled high, images taped to shelves,
not taking for granted this box
of matches, nor candles whittled
down to nub of wicks.

No, not while the rose-colored sandstone lamp
from the shaft at Lascaux hangs above
my desk. Pleistocene artists used flint
& deer fat to light cave walls,
that complex difficulty.

The implement is etched with signs.
Most important of which the long, median line running the entire length
of handle is earth itself. Above the earth,
diagonal lines mimic a flock of birds
flying, herd of bison walking.

Below: a school of fish teems
in the abstract.
Close to the flame a subtle portrait of the artist
faintly sculpted under his or her
thumbprint.

Painting This with a Charcoal Stick

No, not surprising to find
Olson equating the cave with our own
internal "maze," our bodies with geography,
say kidneys as sea, or spine as mountain range,
brain as Arctic, coccyx Antarctic, heart solar system,
lung valley of breath, preferring stone, wood, clay to iron,
brick, steel, glass, copper, or plastic, those basics to any manmade
transformation, & feeling inside himself there in the cave, or geography,
creatures that came before us,
horses rearing up.

Homeland

Surrounded myself with sources including imagery drawn
by Carl Jung himself, kept in a large, red-leather bound
folio for years in a bank vault in Zurich. Scanned in
2008 by the California-based DigitalFusion,
& published by Norton the next year, it
documents his struggle with internal
demons, turned into art on the page.
I, too, am in the cave of my own
being, that which Olson terms
Ethos, Cave of Being.

In the Gratwick Highlands Tapes
Olson harps on the point that one needs
an object of attention so that metaphor ceases,
& the object *becomes once more what it really is,*
the seat & as it were homeland *of our thoughts.*

I chose an archaeological object from here in Maine.
It comes from an area where there is evidence of the hunt.
Defined as a Late Archaic stemmed spear point, comparatively
large at just under six inches in length & three inches wide, it dates
from 3,900-3,000 BP. Made of felsite, native to Maine, although also
known as a Susquehanna point because of resemblance to spear points
in southern New England, indicating that others migrated from there to Maine
during the Late Archaic.

Bison once roamed this very ground,
along with musk ox, elk, mammoth.
Concentration on this spear point
with its sharp edge & added
barb brought on more
archetypal dreams
last night, when
the tide rolled
out leaving
a myriad
of ancient
evidence on
the sea floor,

(Olson says, *that the archetype is the hidden secret of something which is quantity...*)

including: a trunked animal
in stone; a cow's head; a shaft
in the shape of a woman draped
in a blanket; a small fish hammered
out of silver; etc., everything there on
the sea floor alive, animated, shimmering
as if in answer to a Vision Quest, or Jung hallucinating
his imagery into Art, or Olson on LSD giving such attention
to the object before him in the present that it turns into archetext:
*The two things that you'd want to say about an archetext is that it tells
a story, or has the character-action of a story, and that it has the character-
object of the image. These are the two big powers that one deals with in, say, words...*

In Lieu of Solutrean Oil Lamps

What with that grand, full first
day of summer lollygagging
its hours away yesterday,
dawn to dusk, & beyond,
today's in stark contrast
with rain pelting down,
darkness surrounding
us like walls of a cave,
indoors suffering
under Northern
dampness.

That's what I want.
What I'll do. In lieu
of Solutrean oil lamps,
I'll light a few candles against
the dark & dampness & simply draw
the animals have touched me in the study
of the Pleistocene: woolly mammoth I dreamt of;
bison; horse; whale; & apart from them, sketch
the involute wings of this gorgeous Io moth
just stumbled upon in pages of an ancient
volume, as if she'd up & circled
eternally round the flame.

Our Humble Abode

Our humble abode
squeezed in between
two mammoth Victorians,
one of which connects to a barn
formerly used as livery for horse
& carriage at the funeral parlor across
the street. Squeezed in between two monstrous
structures that block the light, prevent snow from
melting, their owners aren't content with what they
have, but keep on building addition after addition, or
remodeling like third-grade homework. That's just it: our
humble abode does more than merely house us, as if we live
in the ur-form of home Tristan Tzara desired in his architecture,
contrasting it to any masculine, castrative, phallic reach: the feminine,
intrauterine examples of cave & yurt, cradle & tomb, or humble Maine Cape.

The Malleable Clay

Not long after portraying her
with having the imaginative ability to fly
with the Great Blue Heron,
or join a flock of egrets
resting in a tree,
than I'll reach out
to the sixth-century BC
terra-cotta Aphrodite mounted
on a swan, or even earlier
Mycenaean Tree Goddess
"in bird epiphany"
from Crete,
as a means of molding
the present & millennia
into the malleable clay
of Timelessness.

One's Visceral Aesthetic Like a Burin Scar

Trekking from Conduché, straddling serpentine
Celé River, no more than a meter deep on one side,
thousand-foot cliffs on the other, breathtaking enough,
but nearing Cabrerets found a field ploughed & ready for
planting among its previous crop of flints, while at the side
of the road noticed the fish made of limestone I'd a premonition
of just before leaving DC.

Busses filled with tourists buzzed
past on the main drag, not giving a damn
for our safety, nor health, fumes combined
with the hot breeze of speed.

Crowds of people got to the cave
of Pech Merle long before us, a limit set
on the number of visitors allowed in the cave.
So after hours of waiting showed powers-that-be
my ID from the National Gallery of Art, stating I'd come
there to write. Ten minutes later escorted in with a much smaller
group than we'd seen enter the grotto in droves, a dozen in our party,
at most. Picasso got it right when he said no one ever painted anything
better.

Of course, the now extinct Dappled Horses weighing in at 25,000 years BP
are comparable to anything at the later caves of Lascaux or Altamira,
but that fish in red from the pike family of the nearby river riding
the back of one of the horses sends chills down the spine.
Timelessness infiltrates the air there. Footprints &
handprints, anonymous signatures.

There's a difference in experiencing the Art here,
say, than in the museum, where I worked back home.
It registers inside one as an immediate aura, a change
in one's being. Lines making mammoth, auroch, horse
etch one's visceral aesthetic like a burin scar. One becomes
one with the Wounded Man. We weren't the same on the long
trek back. A newfound calm in her as she stripped down & stretched
out on the rocky bottom of the Celé River, while at the way station waiting
for the bus to Cahors, I savored the Black Wine of France as never before.

The Wounded Man

Aviform sign hovering above the Wounded Man
at the cave of Pech Merle is none other than
a vulture. Red is the color of writing, life,
& gestation itself, says Olson. I think of
Rimbaud as Wounded Man, who
saw the letter I as the color red
& another.

With Barely a Sign

High dark clouds above
this morning pulled down
the overnight dream, where alone
in the boat the black-water waves
were high & rough with barely a sign
of white-water breaking,
but traversable in my lonely craft.

Ah. There it is, the message
of the dream, where writing is equal
to navigating (I could not see the type
of vessel buoyed me up)
the unknown.

So when the high water
suddenly gave way to shallows
& rugged, rocky shoals,
I grew concerned, wary,
aware of the shoreline in the distance,
& struggled
physically gut to thigh to neck,
arms & rowing shoulders
leaning into waves & away from jutting spars
(woke to call them molars
in the mouth
of the sea).

Recall living to tell the story
in the dream to none other
than the dead,

making these daytime clouds above
readily negotiable for clear sailing ahead.

1644 & 1646

1644 & 1646, Park Avenue addresses,
the papers said, *music*
linked the two.
As did poverty, hunger, & circumstances
of one's birth.
Spanish Church & piano store, respectively.
Respectfully: no more.

Gas leak, which TV crews said,
could be ignited
by the slightest spark, even
a cellphone, blew
windows out,
all the walls
down.

Revealing
slender railroad apartments
on four floors above the 1646 piano shop,
three over the 1644 church.
A style of architecture begun
mid-nineteenth century, when such rooms
housed new arrivals.

Not unlike these
people
from Ecuador, Mexico, Greece, Russia, Puerto Rico,
you know.

Wonder how this particular tragedy calls out
from among so many we hear, see, read about every day?
Other than, at core, language wants its own say
about what was said: that
flat-out demand,
the mythological,
the inferno.

Absolute Piano
owned by Kaoru Muramatsu,
who came to New York from Japan to study art,
met Carl Demler, owner of Beethoven Pianos in Midtown,
& rented an apartment in his Upper East Side building;
married & divorced; 1646 Park Avenue,
part of the settlement.

First listed as missing, she was not
in the building
at the Time.

(Anachronistically, 50 years earlier in the great film
The Pawnbroker,
Rod Steiger, in shame & anguish, drove
a slender steel spike of the receipt stand straight
through his hand.
Imaginary pawnshop set
here at 1642 Park Avenue, East Harlem.)

Friends & relations waiting on
the fate of Griselda Camacho, named
Peace Officer of the Year in 2010 by Hunter College,
worked as a security guard.

Andreas Panagopoulos's body
will be shipped
back to Greece.

Rosaura Hernández Barrios never late, never
missed a day
at her job as a line cook at Triomphe in the Iroquois Hotel,
while on the floor of the piano store a maze of over twenty uprights
in a momentary implosion of music kept one anonymous man
under a crescendo of those labyrinthine walls
safe to tell about it.

To Make the Piece Even Quieter

One can hear it, the solemnity,
of the week
~~has~~ ~~over~~ ended,
& the racket of the ruthless
& secular ~~is~~ barreling down on us on all eighteen
wheels full load
in the rig spewing diesel.
I hear it.
~~But~~ close all windows &
doors, turn Venice
Classical Radio
on with its mix
of Schubert Schumann
& Bach, ~~&~~ not a single
commercial. She's silent
in her study.
I write longhand.
Cross out a few words
to make the piece even quieter.

Mourning the Massacre in the Form of a Woman Weeping

In the seventh & final state of his masterwork, *Guernica,*
Picasso turns the head of the Warrior upward to face the Bull.
Yet, a full seven months after, he's still mourning the massacre
by Fascist & Nazi planes of the ancient Basque town in the form
of a woman weeping. It's right here at the Fogg in Cambridge, black
wash & ink on paper: she's biting her handkerchief in an agonized curse
at the sky. Her image is a visual translation of the artist/poet's own curse
against Franco: *flames bite its lips at the wound-cries of children, cries of
women cries of birds cries of flowers cries of timbers and of stones cries of
bricks cries of furniture of beds of curtains of pots of papers cries of odors which
claw at one another cries of smoke pricking the shoulder...* The Bull is straight out
of Altamira. Russell Martin claims the dead were direct descendants of Cro-Magnon,
while Guy Davenport reports that at the turn of the Twentieth Century,
while Abbé Breuil was drawing his version of the animals
there at Altamira, a young Pablo crawled in with him.
Which would have given him the same perspective
as the supine Warrior, & courage enough to say,
Painting... is an instrument of war.

Iron & Steel

It's there in clear, smooth Japanese cruising waters that Ahab summons the blacksmith's skill to help fashion his own harpoon. Although he'll hammer the pike head himself, he recruits Perth to add unused razors as barbs.

Yet Ahab won't let him cool the iron down in water, preferring what he calls *the true death-temper*, ordering pagan blood drawn from each harpooner, Tashtego, Queequeg, & Daggoo.

This chapter always reminds me of my father's five long years in the Navy, where he sailed into not so clear, smooth Japanese waters, but dodged Kamikazes in order to transport troops between Philippine & East China Seas at Okinawa.

As a kid I'd often rifle through his top bureau drawer just to find the Navy-issued dagger, remove it from scabbard, run eyes & fingers down the heavy steel blade, & marvel.

Sketch

Even as I keep my balance amid the whirling daily existence,
a piece of flesh, an appendage, a stray hair, a sidelong glance,
a drive attempting articulation, a button, the nail of a finger,
a tear, a memory gotten over fully, returning in disguise,
desire unkempt, a breath, an intuition refusing to call itself
knowledge, a dream recollection as real as any thump on the skull,
a dénouement in the decibel of noise not paid attention to
until it lowers with pleasure, an open wound, a war, a torture,
an obituary, a color lost from reminiscence of standing in front
of Rothko or van Gogh, the intimacy experienced once & only
once with a stranger in youth in a foreign country, say Capri,
notes piled up reading Proust, or those dug down into by the beginning
chord of a Bach *Prelude*, love's avowal & hate's renunciation,
dead cells, an emerging desire in the form of disorder, any one
of these things will reach out from the balance of the center
of whirling daily existence to hug at, or leap beyond bounds
of an internal centrifugal force hurled into the World.

In the Room with Brassaï

A matter of lineage, of being in the presence
of it, say, the reason for long-held, deep affection
for Brassaï. In the same room with him in 1976, he spoke
of the secret Paris of the Thirties he knew of & documented
so beautifully offbeat underground carnal perverse black & white.
To be in his presence is to touch Henry Miller, who said Brassaï
was the eye of Paris, could take everything in at the same time,
yet focus with an uncanny ability to interpret lives of pebbles
on the beach. Or Picasso himself with whom he'd spent so
many days & nights at the studio & in the streets. I'm
thinking of his recollection of meeting the man who
manufactured paint for Picasso for twenty years,
when in 1943 he showed Brassaï the artist's
latest list spelled out in his own hand.

It's Joy to read into which Brassaï saw Rimbaud's *Vowels*:
White, permanent, *long line drawn to the edge of the page*_____
silver_____
Blue, cerulean_____
cobalt_____
Prussian_____
Yellow, cadmium lemon (light) _____
Madder lake, bitumen_____
...
Black, ivory_____
Ochre, yellow and red_____
...
Raw umber, natural and burnt_____
...

Terra rosa, natural and burnt_____

...

There, in the room listening to Brassaï;
in the brothel talking with Henry;
in the cave silent with Picasso.

Li Po Waiting for Orders to Write

The image
of that lone
(not lonely – the oarsman
has a companion, or two,
depending on how one
interprets
the ink) boat
in Cha Shih-Piao's *River
Landscape in Rain*, naturally
(if not haphazardly)
drives me back an entire millennium
to Li Po's, *The River Song*,
where the poet
has wine
enough
for a thousand cups.
Kutsu's prose song
hangs there
from a scroll,
while Li Po waits
for orders
from the Emperor
to write.

When Li Po Writes from the Perspective of the Sailor's Wife

When Li Po writes
from the perspective
of *The Sailor's Wife*,
as the subtitle reads
in his book I bought
for a dollar, & jotted
down my own quick
phrases on blank pages
in the back, or which Pound
calls a *Letter* in his translation,
the Feminine angle is something
to behold.

She's shy at first
glance & pouts like the kid
she was, when marrying him at fourteen.
By fifteen he has her crack a smile
for the first time in his presence,
as if a veil lifted. His absence
causes thoughts of death,
& signs of age appear
prematurely.

The man writes
in a such a manner
that by the time she's
sixteen, worrying she's already
past her prime, one can *hear* the tone
of voice projected by this abject adolescent.

Random History with Vermeer Spans Decades

Beauty moves as color
moves, radiance a secret
frequency upon the eye, or
as music will, corporeal timbre
against the inner ear. Proust had
Vermeer in mind, when singling out
the tiny splotch of yellow the painter
placed upon a wall in Delft, seeing it
separately, as something self-enclosed,
equating it to some Chinese calligraphic
message, just as he'd done before in the novel
with the small musical phrase from Vinteuil's sonata.

Vermeer's surfaces:
anything but superficial.
Interiors filled with immediacy
& extended time flowing down
toward our own here & now.

In May 1921 Proust leaves the house
for the last time, having read news articles
about an exhibition of paintings from den Haag
including, *View of Delft* & *Girl with a Pearl Earring*.
He struggled to get to the Jeu de Paume, needing help
walking from a companion. I'm not sure of any importance
in the coincidence that the same two paintings stood out to me
at a similar Dutch exhibition at the Le Petit Palais in Paris in 1987?

But that same year I stumbled
on the essay, *Giotto's Joy*,
in which Kristeva suggests
that color escapes our internal
censorship. Ah, then, how Beauty
moves as color moves, radiance
a secret frequency upon the eye,
or as music will, corporeal timbre
against the inner ear.

My own random history with Vermeer spans
decades, beginning in 1974, when on a cross-country
road trip we parked next to the fenced-in hole in the ground,
which would become the East Wing of the National Gallery of Art,
& where sixteen years later I'd work in the library.

On that beautiful day in April on the first leg
of our 5-month journey down to Mexico,
where color viscerally erupts,
we ran into the West Wing,
where in all seriousness
the only thing I carried
out of Washington, DC
was the red
of *The Girl with the Red Hat*
(Meisje met de rode hoed) c. 1665-1667.
The model for it not actually a girl, but manikin.
A wooden *tronie* wearing clothes. It made no difference,
because Vermeer's red alone escaped all internal censorship,
& Beauty moved all the way to Veracruz, as color moves, radiance
a secret frequency upon the eye, or as music will, corporeal timbre against
the inner ear.

As haunted as I was by that red, the real girl
of *Girl with the Pearl Earring* also followed me
out of Paris. There's Vermeer in miniature near the open
window reflected in the jewel. That's his desire. To be inside.
He'd paint her naked, if he had the chance. Don't take my word
for it, but inspect as close as possible the copper pan hanging in the corner
of the back wall in *Woman Pouring Milk*, & you'll find the feminine anatomical
flesh, naked & sturdy as Rembrandt's *Bathsheba at Her Bath* in the Louvre.

Vermeer adds an old satyr gazing up at her,
as well as a younger, handsome black courtier.
Love is what we have so often placed in front of us
by Vermeer. Love of color. Love of Beauty. Ovid wrote
books on Love. It was the aura of *Girl with the Pearl Earring*,
who followed me out of Paris, & whose visage I had in mind, when
turning to see what Ovid had to say about the color of his beloved's clothes.

No, Ovid has no use for gold.
Cares not one iota for Tyrian purple.
Wants other colors that cost less money.
"Why carry all your fortune on your back?"
He wants azure blue like a clear sky, when wind
ceases to bring rain from the South. Desires yellow,
the color of the ram of the sun Aphrodite required Psyche
to fetch as one of her labors toward individuation. The turban
on the head of the real girl with the pearl earring is of that blue &
yellow bypassing our internal censor, fashioned by the artist's hand
into Beauty that moves as these colors move, radiance a secret frequency
upon the eye, or as music will, corporeal timbre against
the inner ear.

There are days this winter, when there is nothing
but snow as far as the eye can see. White, no other color.
A brutal absence. So when this woman, the one embroidering
small animals for the granddaughter expected to arrive into this world
next month, (reminding me of Vermeer's *Lacemaker* at the Louvre), sent
a postcard of *Girl Reading a Letter by an Open Window*, (colors saved
from the firestorm at Dresden), it became the path Beauty takes when
it moves as color moves, radiance a secret frequency upon the eye,
or as music will, corporeal timbre against the inner ear.
In the middle of winter. Above a field of snow. No
other color. A brutal absence. Words on the back
of the postcard subtle & loving as the reflection
of the girl in the window, or those shadows,
also coming toward one, that Vermeer
added to the blank back wall.

Quiet Drama

Before 5:00 in the morning the moon drew her
closer, where in her admiration for it, full as it is
in May, I caught their spiritual embrace. Flower Moon
she knew well enough to call it, as if she were one opening
from the ground up, or mouth down. A beautiful interaction,
quiet drama. It seemed part of a Noh play, dressed as she was to
the nines, preparing to meet new colleagues after flying out this early
today, down to the District of Columbia, getting that much closer to her
Full Flower Moon in the meantime.

The Train Stub

Love finding train stubs or plane tickets, museum
passes in between pages of books I take down randomly
from the shelf to read in addition to the volume's contents,
carrying me back to that pleasurable time of travel, harnessing
it like a slow dray horse to the present.

In this particular case, Amtrak takes us back, pre-holiday,
to Boston & the Beacon Hill Hotel on Charles, where we walked
through brittle air from the station, December light already fading
by late afternoon, up Joy Street, down Chestnut, amid the rich's attempts
to outdo one another, mansion-to-mansion, by way of decoration, to the hotel.

We felt as free, & ungainly, with our luggage plus another bag with coats
for our daughter & granddaughter, the real reason for the getaway, as a pair
of web-footed wood ducks wobbling across a stretch of ice to what open water
there was left on the river, settling in in the smallest room they had with glasses
of red wine. Look at her golden aura too good not to return to here & now,

enhanced by the confines of the walls, which won't let that energy disperse,
& sunset melting down Charles Street just as all the electric lights go on,
a veritable lost Vermeer, recently rediscovered in an attic room in Delft.
Train stub marks a poem by Rolf Jacobsen describing his own wife's visage
waking up above her sewing machine, fallen asleep on the task of the yellow
dress, calling her up from her past to his present in which she no longer exists.

One of Those Days

One of those days
when there is no difference between the beauty
of the world & the need for language,
between light of the dream,
its tender, gentle
characters,
perhaps the dead,
& the daylight one has
to get up in to make a living.

Her flesh next to me is nothing less
than a refuge & a sentence.
The breath of talk,
the plan for today
amid the realization that living in the moment
retains vast expanses of memory.
Memory & the present moment.

Fill the air
with Rachmaninoff's *Song Op. 21, No. 7*,
sung by Anna Netrebko. Our own mouths
sipping coffee, sharing everything
in exchange of minor words
& silences.
"Stay safe," our parting phrase
heading toward respective workday worlds,

where the snow-covered world possesses an added interior:

what Benjamin might call the aura,

or Goethe the thing of beauty in the veil.

Sky's magnificent cathedral clouds.

The lonely, thin, hooded figure walking the well-worn path of the homeless

toward public facilities

so early in the morning bringing everything back down to earth.

But why the image of the tanker, *Torgovy Bridge*, rises up

before me long before reaching the harbor

is a mystery that can only be explained

away by the earlier recollection

of when I was captive

at the factory job

with the only

window

facing the only spruce,

the apparatus of the machine timing my every move,

in full control of my existence,

the film of the memory

of Venice

passing

before me then,

vision of *Torgovy Bridge*

transporting me somewhere else today.

Sunflowers

Sunflowers in the front of the house
kitchen bay window.

I drift out back where the other sun
ensconces itself in an April sky.

Humble sunflowers more help these past
few days than that proud star.

Universe of Words

The world's not in need
of anything else.
From this perspective, at least, starting
with the sounds of mourning
doves & hammer blows.

Between days of rain
a spider constructed a one-lane highway
across the old rosebush past the deck
to the wrought-iron table
I'm writing on.

I just witnessed a whimsical chevron
of terns winging north.
The crowd of jonquils next door far outnumber
the lone flower my wife flashed a smile
of pride over earlier this morning.

A female blackbird shivering
tail-feathers in a brief fertility rite
before & after the male lights.
More spider wires billowing.
Green shadows.

Maple buds, bare linden, & erratic mimosa
branches I know only from memory.
Cold coffee, & desire, desire
to speak, to write, to reassemble
the entire world according

to pulse & sap, blood & history,
dirt stone bark cloth skin
shoot web sound urge
bent thrust universe
of words.

Uccello in the Process of Unveiling

Vasari was hard
on Uccello, condemning him for painting stones red,
casks' lack of perspective, giving movement to
one side only of an English Captain's horse,
which he said in reality would make
the horse topple over.

Topple over, horse!
Amazing how reputations change over centuries.
Dorn said Olson was a teacher the equal of Euripides.
Baudelaire claimed his humiliations his graces,
& that: *A succession of small acts of will*
achieve a large result.

Vasari complained
of the vast number of trunks of small studies left by Uccello,
diminishing their value in his eyes in favor of larger works in oil.
The critic puts down the artist's obsession with perspective,
& while we know the modern preference for a flat plane,
chaos reigns supreme in Uccello's, *Battle of San Romano*,
where no correct perspective would do
the conflict justice.

Seemed a strange, yet benevolent coincidence,
that I'd been thinking of my friend,
Peter Anastas, who studied
in Florence as a young man,
when Vasari's chapter on Paolo Uccello
was the sole page marked in my old paperback,

a book that somehow emerged after realigning my library.

Vasari ends his criticism
of Uccello with an anecdote
of the painter covering up a work in progress
commissioned for the space above the door at the church
of San Tommaso.

Donatello, inquiring as to the nature of its subject, was told
to wait & see.

Later, Donatello found Uccello in the process of unveiling:
Thomas reaching into the wound.

Instead of praising the work, Donatello commented that now
that Uccello was showing it to the world,
it should rather have remained covered.

Deeply humiliated,
Uccello retreated
to house & studio.

Vasari underestimated
Uccello's actual death
date by over fifty years.

Going Near

Felt it held a lot of meaning, the simple phrase uttered
in the middle of the night in the dream,
Going near.

To what? Soul flesh truth other?
How? Walking flying speaking kissing?
When? Yesterday tomorrow eternally?

Now, certainly. In what manner?
Oracularly simply raucously thoughtfully?
Then what? Examine fondle enjoy leave alone?

Rites of Passage

The rarity
of say three days running
the weight of misery
hunches the shoulders
while reading
over those who've
gone before over
poetry's sharp shoals
so you don't have time
to jot down
a single word
to match that
misery.
It remains silent.
Unaccounted for
for three days
running,
but the getting
through somehow
proves the worth
of such silence
in those rare
instances
against what
would have been
some bleak amateur
wailing.
To reiterate:
the misery

Suppose if I were
if the mind were
born or trained
that way, then
I would once
conceiving of a
thought try to
ratchet it up
into a lofty
conception,
but it doesn't,
it's not, it won't,
which other is a mere
tramping upon
solid ground like
Ireland or Gloucester
for that matter
reaching down to
ancestors in my
continuing immediacy,
or foreign, say
Venice where it's
not so much solid
ground, but porous
waters buried tree
trunks & basilica
ceilings mimicking
the sky above them.
No, what happens is

of three days running
deserves nothing
other than a stoic
resilience
dredged from its
depths.

no formal conception,
but an informal
spontaneous, rhythmic
reenactment of
the here & now
of experience
in language.
Sentences with
boots on, letters
shibboleths in rites
of passage.

Nonetheless, Enraptured

She said that's what she disliked about headstones,
as we toured the cemetery
for exercise: that names
wear down, & even
disappear.

Which differed so radically from my take, we had to smile
the smile of complete *différance*, alive as Hell,
& in Joy, spring cool the way
I like, ten degrees too low
for her, but nonetheless,
enraptured.

The drive is a defense, after all, & a passion, a will,
lingual, to delve, uncover perhaps
without revealing totally,
an inscription, name
on stone,

which when I imagine it, is torn open forcefully to make the stone
another force, say, Noguchi's, *Great Rock of Inner Seeking*,
brailed so often during lunch hours off
from the drudgery of hours of work,
or this fish stone I knew I'd find
along the way to Pech Merle.

We are water & mineral stone.
Inscribed with a secret name,
not our own, but anonymously,
weighed in the hands
of Thoth, or Justice
in a blindfold.

Those Shadows Across the Way

Those shadows across the way,
beyond the stockade fence, against
both houses' clapboards, pink & green,
are brand new in spring sun, & trembling,
bare tree limbs in March wind.

Snow banks in retreat. As am I: working
on limiting my desire for anything
other than what is here within
my immediate purview:
weathervane pointing
west under cloudless
sky, Paris visible
in the distance.

What Is It There Inside?

By the time
I got to Picasso's
former Paris studio
on rue des Grands Augustins
it was a fine bookstore, so I'll try
to imagine as best I can the scene on
Christmas Eve in 1943*, when the artist
unveiled a series of palm-sized, bronze Venuses.

Brassaï reports the presentation includes
a loving stroke of the tiny breasts by the same
hands that made them, while the sculptures themselves
remind Brassaï of Balzac's *Preface* to **The Magic Skin**
in which the novelist says that a truly philosophical writer
has the uncanny ability *to see the object to be described, either
because the object comes to them, or because they themselves go
toward the object.*

What is it there inside the writer,
sculptor, or Aurignacian painter, other
than his, or her own *awe* to match in language,
stone, or ochre, the raw material of the object at hand?

*Brassaï finishes his report without failing to note *this sinister year of 1943.*

The Drive In

The drive in
& deep down
so pages split
apart from spine.
All the talk of rocks,
house of myth, secret
& sacred, brought me
vertically to the apex
of the ledge, where I saw
the ancient Bison herded off
the cliff, & suddenly surprised,
additionally, by what recent stone
steps up there revealed: shell midden,
good distance from where they gathered,
as Olson intimated on the ramp extended out
in order to eat them raw, or horizontally, during
my own lunch break from the lowly library job in DC,
out only to admire & caress Noguchi's *Great Rock of Inner
Seeking*.

Bataille & my dovetailing
of his *Sorcerer's Apprentice*
with Olson's *THE AREA, and
the Discipline*, in which they both
accentuate the need for precise attention
to the totality of things, the despair of the mass

of men ending as spokes in the grinding corporate
wheel, as opposed to launching the risk life is to be oneself,
or find satisfaction in a significant kiss, or her naked on the bed.

One Must Crawl on One's Belly

Appropriately enough, in order to observe both the bison
& vulva carved in clay at the *grotte de Bédeilhac*,
Ariège, Midi-Pyrénées, France, one must crawl
on one's belly. Jean Clottes claims its technique
differs from the bison at *Le Tuc d'Audoubert*,
in that here the imagery is molded by hand.
Clottes marvels at the anatomical details,
whereby the mons is built up into pubic
triangle, & the vulva cleft embellished
with a concretion forming the clitoris.

Strange, how when I saw it
I thought how it differed, as well,
& greatly from Tiepolo's 18th century
painting in the Museum of Fine Arts in Boston,
Time Disrobing Truth, in which the artist dares not
bring Truth round fully frontal, & as Kristeva points out:
Truth has her right leg where her left should be, and this leg
is thrust forward, between herself and the genitals of Time,
Time with raptor's wings, & a snarl at Eros, whose quiver
of arrows is tossed to the floor, Love defenseless against
Time, although the Magdalenian clay vulva as Truth
seems to outwit It.

Iron Bars of Ballast Tell a Story

One morning, a Sunday, you're walking along with the sound
of Nina Simone's voice singing, *Black is the Color*
of My True Love's Hair, picking out threads,
traces, hints, remnants of Slaves'
lamentations.

Ironically, she loves
the ground he goes on,
the land, which sadly, is
not African.

Twenty-four hours later, need one say, dreaded
Monday, you get wind of a sunken Slave ship dredged
up off the Cape of Good Hope, where only the iron bars
of ballast tell the story: In April, 1794, the Portuguese, *São José*,
left Lisbon with 1,500 iron blocks of ballasts bound for Mozambique
to pick up its human cargo of over 400, to captain & crew, nameless Slaves.

There, in that wind you're getting word of
sunken Slave ship is the sound of a voice along
with sirens & protests, smashed windows past iron
bars: it's Baltimore blowing up for good & no reason
other than that of those 12,000,000 people sold into bondage,
& lost names in the wind.

You get word of copper
fastenings & sheathing used
to keep slaves tied on their backs
in the bottom of the hold, while 1,500

iron bars of ballast balance the weight of between
400-500 human beings, who move, ever so slightly,
are not as stable as tubs of molasses. You hear Nina sing:

Hard times in the city
in a hard town by the sea
ain't nowhere to run to there
ain't nothin' here for free…

It's a long story
iron bars of ballast tell.
Iron bars of ballast tell a story
clanging like the resounding noise
of a cell door slamming.

Think of Detroit

For some reason, when I think of Detroit
I think of art, Diego & Frida,
not cars.

A municipality,
18 billion in debt,
bankrupt,

with only its art collection left
as anything
of value.

Catalyst Acquisitions
& Bell Capital Partners
interested in purchasing the entire collection

for $1.7 billion.
Beijing Poly International Auction Company
wants the Asian collection.

There was the Rivera ink drawing
at a gallery in Mexico City
wanted to take out a loan

of ten grand for
in the summer
of 1974.

Or the Rivera portrait of Manuel's father,
former Minister of Cultural Affairs,
hanging in the living room,

where we were poor
houseguests
in servants' quarters.

She said, "Every line in a poem is an autobiography."
He said, "We are called on to correct all economies."
Tawdry poet's clothes, jacket lining torn

in disarray, so little any longer fit.
Detroit now offering free houses
for writers to return to the city.

When I think of Detroit I think of my own crimes
& pride in ragged clothes & fingerprints cops
can't lift because they've worked

hard on keyboards at getting life down down
down to where I can stand on my own
seven wounds & listen to the chorus

of internal organs.
Frida stood on the border between Mexico
& United States in pink muslin dress smoking,

Ford automobile plant spewing out carbon
dinosaur footprints in the sky enough
to blot out Old Glory.

She holds a tiny Mexican flag in symbolic comparison.
I crossed the border at Mexicali & got close to Frida
there that night in Oaxaca

when Manuel Avila Camacho told of being at Casa Azul,
when Frida cooked & served lunch all by herself,
telling stories of the integrity of Trotsky,

ragged ass of Breton inside baggie pants,
her love of color while arranging flowers,
& childhood happiness before the accident.

In my own way then beholding both Fridas
at the museum in paint & blood & here
in Oaxaca in flesh as word.

Carlos Fuentes said, "Mexico is a country that
has been made by its wounds." I see Frida
straddling the border between Mexico

& United States at the foot of Detroit, bleaker than bleak,
or stretched out at Henry Ford Hospital with DETROIT
spelled out as the last word on the iron bed flying.

Frida in fragments, umbilicaled to miscarried
fetus, pelvis, snail, torso, steel dispenser,
& purple orchid, above brown earth

into blue sky. Ford plant dead in the Dearborn distance.
Desolate Detroit with its 16th century Bruegel estimated
by Christie's for salivating creditors at two hundred million dollars.

The Wedding Dance, as if some civic divorce
could come between the city of Detroit & its art & land
in the hands of the greedy who see only dollar signs rather than

aggregate joy of village dancers portrayed by Pieter Bruegel the Elder.
Seriously, an economics professor from Cornell University took time
to estimate that were Detroit Institute of Arts privatized

the cost of viewing *The Wedding Dance* alone would be
twelve thousand dollars an hour per person, &
although apologizing for his formulation,

the apology was not for crassness of its lack of aesthetic,
but for "the crudeness of these approximations."
When I think of Detroit I see the word *riot*

swirling around in the final syllable & of 1967,
when cops busted the United Community for Civic Action
offices above the printing shop on 12th Street unlicensed to serve

alcohol, & all Hell broke loose.

When I think of Detroit I think of the word *ghetto*
& origin of the word in Venice in the 17th century, based
on the Italian for *foundry*, where that city's Jews congregated.

When I think of Detriot (sic, just came out that way!)
I think of impoverishment & how wealth accumulated at one pole
produces misery, ignorance, slavery, & brutalization at the opposite.

Diego's mural of Detroit's industry begins on the East Wall,
where he originally planned to paint a beet bulb as rooted kernel
of truth, but after Frida's miscarriage, replaced that image with an infant

protected by earth goddesses & abundance from the land of plenty: pumpkins,
squash, eggplant, apples, plums, etc. West Wall fresco rises above the Latin phrase
carved in marble, *Vita Brevis Longa Ars*, depicting man & turbine, work & production,

a dove & symbolic opposite the hawk.
Passenger planes vs. warplanes.
Hammer & star.

The North Wall holds monumental sculptural figures
based on Mesoamerican Chacmool models down
to predella panels depicting workers' lives

at the Rouge River plant punching the clock
through the rest of the daily grind, while center
fresco shows man as yet another machine making engines

& transmissions for the 1932 Ford V-8 fully formed in its final stage.

South Wall's dizzying assembly of axels, steering wheels, hoods, trunks,
chassis, all observed as spectacle by a passive group of tourists.
It's back on the North Wall that Diego portrays himself

as sad & poor as Charlie Chaplin
in black bowler
hat.

When I think of Detroit I think of poverty & tragedy, not comedy.
Of what led to the bankruptcy of the city, after borrowing
money to pay for workers' pensions, & how creditors

like Bank of America & UBS made out like bandits
entering into contracts with the municipality called
"interest rate swaps" in 2005.

Wall Street-driven crash the next year decimated
the pension fund, & banks called for millions.
($300 million extracted from citizenry.)

To think of Detroit calls up the image of someone bereft of any form
of personal or economic Freedom, those in prison, or homeless
beggar with mendicant, saintly, obstinate face.

We Took Time Away from the World

We took time away from the world
a number of times.
Stood among ageless stones
with a voice all their own.
Took a ferry to nowhere
for no reason.
Stepping into an ancient church
shaped like a ship
upside-down,
where six parishioners
watched three priests
perform the ritual,
& one African accent
read the story
of the crucifixion
from the gospel
according to St. John.
It's awfully important
to take time away
from the world
in order to hear
the heartbeat of
the otherworldly.

Spanish Moss

No sooner
than dropping her off at the airport,
the house wilts
by absence.
Coffee's still on
in the dark morning.
Read the Sunday *Times*
regarding culture's inability
to address current political chasms.
There's a creaking & moaning about
the house in its loss. Home gets homely.
Shabby & small.

Later, I'll turn
on the old movie channel
just to pass Time, slowed to a crawl.
Sounder is on. Watch the boy walk
alone with dog past southern
trees with hanging Spanish
moss, & at first think of her
down there in Georgia,
but quickly wax toward
the first Time I saw such
vegetation: father's funeral in Florida,
where I had to ask the gravedigger
what it was
called.

Spanish moss
weeping all over
the cemetery. Military
honor guard, including two women
dressed in Navy whites.
The father in the film,
calls out to his son,
finally catching up to him at the edge
of a beautiful, but desolate landscape.
He tells the boy how he survived
the dynamite blast that left him
with that limp.

The dynamite blast rang synchronous
with Kamikaze attacks on Liberty Ships my father experienced,
transporting troops to Okinawa.

The fictional character says he ran as fast as the lightning of God's thought.
My dad could never articulate the trauma,
although many's a Time I shook him
awake from untold nightmares.
Spanish moss reminds me
of a musical instrument playing the vibration,
that is the silence
for an absence.

Lamentation of the World.

Sound of the Equinox

I hear it.

On my wavelength, after all, the Equinox.
Sound of bass or cello brushed
& struck by horsehair,
my lower-rung
register.
Despite cold rain
today approximately
three hours from sun
illuminating both hemispheres at once.

Overnight snow covered over by morning
rain producing bad light makes
no difference to what I hear
as gentle rumbling
coming forth
at the meeting
of both terrestrial & celestial
exactly three hours from now,
(minus two minutes).

This stack of books reveals a certain affection
for renewable sources, for the kind of return
& advance at the same time
the Equinox
in its billions of years
of accumulated experience represents:

some so dog-eared; another back
coverless; & another coverless & back
pages missing!!

One author claims even the thought of a goal
distracts one's attention from the moment.
I'm down with that, with Bach on cello
& Charlie Haden on bass for that
matter in my hearing of the slow,
rushing Equinox making
the fragmented second
& Eternity one.

D. H. Lawrence & the Etruscan Tomb of the Bulls

So I stumble in my search,
or veer,
merely following an internal, hermetic path,
which leads me to an image from the Etruscan
Tomb of the Bulls in Tarquinia
leading to D.H. Lawrence's 1927
visit there, where everything rises up
from the underworld.

Lawrence calls this internal, intuitive path
instinct, pulse in the bloodstream,
throb of the loins, saying
the bull is father
of milk.

Here in the tomb
he finally finds the origin,
nucleus, germ, One
from which All
began.

Lawrence surges
past any moral application
of what might be labeled *pornographica*
here, in the image I've stumbled upon,
where a painted human couple stand fornicating,
while being approached by a hieratic bull, are understood
as embodying true life force
without restrictions,

an image of complete
Freedom.

He sees the process of the art of the Etruscans,
as Olson saw that by Cro-Magnon, first scratching
with a burin, or in this case a nail, the outline
of the figure before filling it in with color.

At the same time Lawrence views
Etruscan works only suggestive of an edge,
not outlined, comparing them to the art of the Chinese.

The dying man envisions the height of life
portrayed in the Tomb of the Bulls
in Tarquinia in 1927.

His **Etruscan Places** will be published five years later,
posthumously.

II.

Immediately after reading Lawrence's take on Etruscan art,
I head down cellar, where behind a book on Pre-Columbian art history,
& **Tula, the Toltec Capital of Ancient Mexico**, I find yet another discard
from the local art school library, one as far as I can see deserving of such Fate,
what with its last borrow date stamped February 1991, its stultified academic language,
dearth of maps & plates, & wealth of useless information.

But, there's value at least in back of the text
in the Glossary of Etruscan words,
where facts speak
for themselves:

matan – before; *Oam* – to place,
to found; *mur* – to be, to live in a place,
murs –urn, sarcophagus; *favin* – temple vault, grave;
tes – to look after, *tesin* – curator; *tus* – funerary niche,
pulia – wife; *sec* – daughter; *hus* – son; *apa* – father, *afrs* – ancestors;
tusuroir – double urn, man & wife; *nuno* – sacrificing; *aper-ucen* - sacred act;
ais – god, *aisna* – divine; *san* – the dead, *santi* – funerary priest; *usil* – sun; *ut* – to give;
paxaour – bacchant; *zic* – to write; *zix* – book; *cel* – point of the compass.

Here, & There

Here, white lilacs
in a cold May. There,
she stands smiling, naked
in less than a foot of the current
running under her in the Celé River.
We're fresh out of the cave of Pech Merle.
Refreshed in a new world out of the cave of Pech Merle.
The Celé River is the clearest water I've seen since the Adriatic
at Split. Her nakedness near blinding after the dark lines outlining
our Dappled Horses in the cave, our sight heightened to make out the form
of the Red Fish of the pike family taken out of this very river as glaciers retreated.

Reminded here,
of there, & of that
heads-up from Michel Leiris
regarding the eschatology of life itself,
that we'll lose all that we love, & knowing this
is why it is necessary that we gather up all that we love,
like the emotion of great farewells, in something of unforgettable beauty.
Come close, Dear One, Foreign One, Friend, let's embrace that place there
twenty-five thousand years & six thousand miles away, & this place, white lilacs
in a cold May, black ocean water with waves marking Time, kissing sand & stone.

Now, & Then

Now, shadow of a crow.
There was no shadow of crow
down there in the cave at Lascaux.
However, the man who took the final
photographs before it closed for good points
out that the cow with her foal on the south wall
of the Axial Gallery has a black underbelly,
which indicates both the animal's winter
coat & shadow from
sun above.

Black & Red

At Lascaux one comes away, tears oneself away, as best one can
from the awe of the power of Black: Bulls & Aurochs; meandering
Black Outlines, Antlers above a series of Black Dots & Rectangles;
Stags' Hooves & Manes; Frieze of Little Horses; Wounds in Pregnant
Horse; never mind fierce tandem of horned Black Bison in courageous
rage.

Black as Masculine.
Black as Power.
Black as Death.

Slowly, however,
one is drawn back
into the subtler awe
of the color Red.

Red as generative.
Red as understanding
continuity of life manifested
in the Feminine, & Writing.

Color, which Kristeva points out
in *Giotto's Joy* is the sole dynamic
bypassing our internal censor.

Red Cow with collar at Lascaux.
Red, as Olson writes, is ground, is Force
to pass Knowledge on, is Woman's Body.

II.

Not to mention the link he makes to the tectiform
upturned curves interpreted as bows of boats
on the walls of the cave at Castillo, whose
latitude is less than one degree

south of his own Gloucester,
where he found reports of a Woman,
(mother, a Maine Micmac, father Newfoundland
Red Beothuk) who remembered traveling in just such

a craft, forecastle holding all belongings
for as long a Voyage of migration need be made,
say in Time, in Millennia, across teeming ice-strewn,
unknown Sea.

What He Sees

Max Raphael asks
about whether, at first,
there was a prohibition against
mixing colors together, thus the earliest
all-black, or entirely red animal figures, until
that taboo relaxed, perhaps over millennia,
when the outline of the body could be
drawn in the concave-convex curve,
& the rest of the form filled in
in red?

He sees Space
between paintings
as a matter of tension,
not only among the animals
themselves, but the Space outside
the cave, where the actual herd may
wander away from half-nomadic hunters.

Olson, too, found Space here
in America, citing Folsom cave,
as vast, a daily challenge to the earliest
to arrive, *sun like a tomahawk*, while the sea
as well, is as vast as the plains themselves, so it's
no surprise the poet alludes to what Melville jots down
in his *Journal up the Straits* that which he sees after passing
Cape Finisterre in Spain with its 42.47 degree coordinate down
to Cape Vincent in Portugal: ...*bold cliff. Cave under light house.*
The whole Atlantic breaks here.

From the Chromatic to the Clear

It's 1985, a few seconds ago
in terms of the subject matter,
but I'm in Salem at the Peabody
Essex Museum, wondering about
the role of color, while discussing
it with William Eldridge curating
the find from Bull Brook, Ipswich,
showing me with scalpel fluted points
found 18 inches down with charcoal: *Black*
in Nez Perce from the word cimu.x for charcoal,
carbon dated at 8,565$\pm$ 285 years before the present.

Three months back
then researching what color
is, does. Cold beginning among
vast shades of grey, the rest heat up.
Yet by the end, Space intervenes when
Stevens' Pennsylvania settlers step out
of color, move from the chromatic to the clear.

The Horse's Ancestors

Woke up from a dream picturing
the head & neck of a contemporary horse,
say American Pharoah or Divining Rod, &
yet a human voice echoing around the image
before the dream closed: *The horse's ancestors
stand behind it.* Drawing it precisely back down
to the cave walls at Lascaux, or even older Chauvet.

Add to the Names of the Great Guides of the Aegean

Add to the names of the great guides of the Aegean,
Homer, Strabo, Pausanias, Odysseas Elytis,
George Seferis, that of Zbigniew Herbert,
who in his essay, *Labyrinth on the Sea*,
examines origin & meaning of Minoan
art on the island of Crete.

He's less than impressed with the more famous frescoes from Knossos,
Dolphins, Parisienne, & *Blue Bird*, weary that first day from his wait
for the ship *Theseus* & overnight journey from Piraeus to Heraklion,
but senses the importance of the stucco relief of the bull in a rage
painted in *dark, burnt red*
turning brown-...

It's the bull at the center of the labyrinth, which will prove key to his
understanding of the ancient civilization. As guide, however, he'll often
mix impressions of art with that of the current culture he finds on the streets.
In what he calls the meat & fruit neighborhood of Heraklion, sits down to a meal
of small fish fried whole, goat cheese, olives, *moussaka, ouzo*, & the white wine
of Samos. But that's only *Prelude* to what he witnesses in a stall across the way.

A butcher puts on a show, quartering an ox, orchestrating with knife & cleaver
deconstruction of once live flesh of heart, haunch, & bone down to fat & meat.
It reminds him of the Hagia Triada sarcophagus he had only minutes with
during his first day on the island at the museum before it closed,
foreshadowing what he'll return to find the next day, & seeing
in this slaughter: *critics who will busy themselves with us,*
who will torture what we leave behind, hacking
& ripping blindly.

II.

This small sarcophagus encapsulates the entire ancient culture the poet seeks
to decipher. It portrays a funeral procession. All figures shown in profile.
A seven-page spread of the imagery here next to me from a book
purchased over forty years ago, published in France in 1964,
shows colors that are rich, figures large & vocal
in their silence. A chariot with green
horses, another with winged-lions.

Zbigniew sees the skirts of the women as colorful bells.
What he sees in person, what's not shown here, even
in the encompassing seven pages, is the sacrifice
of the bull, center of the labyrinth. The bull is
fettered, he says, with throat cut, blood
flowing into a dish. The animal's eyes
are wide open & full of melancholy.

Herbert acknowledges entrance of the god,
mystery of mysteries, the mystical cause...
in the form *of a statue, a herm,*
concrete as stone.

Herbert compares the crypt,
this piece of painted sculpture
to a **Book of the Dead**. Something
that has value as document: *a visual record*
of an ancient tradition. He interprets: double-sided
axe, *lybrys*, root of the word labyrinth; bulls' votive horns;
& musical instruments will signify *a formalized liturgy.*

Zbigniew Herbert, guide to the realm of the dead:

It is a powerful & almost joyful song of resurrection...

Tomorrow Our Soul Sets Sail

Rushing out the door to keep the appointment on time,
grabbed a slender book off the shelf, one I'd forgotten I'd
owned, what with having recently borrowed the collected
work of George Seferis from a friend, half-recalled this little
POEMS bought for $1.95 so long ago. Chose it so it could fit
unobtrusively in my jacket pocket, not wanting to flaunt it
in the dentist's office during the inevitable wait, not wanting
to stare at walls or the other patients. As I read it thought of
Elizabeth Bishop in her aunt's waiting room ready to turn seven
in three days, at the same time experiencing this rush of sudden
consciousness, while questioning what it meant. In Seferis, I found
& identified with his old man on the river bank, whose bloodstream
equals that of the geography. Seferis seems to be wondering just how
to go forward after all the mid-century strife & war. He refuses to grant
thought, feeling, movement, even courage itself as the answer. He finishes
the discourse in similar fashion to Stevens' late-in-life image of something
beyond truth, recollecting an anonymous palm, green leaves of peace rocking
in the wind.

Charles Swann in Black Calligraphic Script

Just before bed
I stumbled upon,
(no, more opening
the book to a page
as if it were a toss
of sticks according
to the rules of chance
in the *I Ching*), Seferis'
poem *Calligraphy*, where
we're introduced to sails on
the Nile in search of a youth
made of marble, one-winged
birds looking for the other, while
the ink is invisible. So I dreamt last night
that I'm outside writing with my own pen,
inscribing the name Charles Swann.

Swann, who tries to convince Odette
that not all poets are scoundrels, although
that's her intractable belief, having known
a woman who fell in love with one who wrote
only *of love, the sky, & the stars*, but did her out
of three-hundred-thousand francs. Swann, who tries
to convince her of the worth of a work of art, or piece
of music, fearing her disillusionment by art might find
the same in that of love.

My nib ran out of ink after writing down the name, Charles Swann, but I still see it there on the Magic Writing Pad in black calligraphic script.

Nothing but Silence

Walk down there.
Just past the birches still
waving goodbye to the glacier.
Talk in low tones. Crouch in the grotto.
Marvel at the Thunderbird, wings spread,
not in flight, but dance. He sidles up next the Moon
Woman, stark naked, subtle rump, possibly gravid belly,
splay of crotch & thigh. Nothing but Silence. Eternity in lines.

"Moose was Whale Once," Said Old John Neptune

In this way
I've been out at sea
the past couple of months
recording imagined travels across
Atlantic, Aegean, Mediterranean, Pacific,
& Adriatic waters, ports as diverse as Heraklion,
Nantucket, Okinawa, Venice, & Boston.

Hard to fathom
the years-long whaling
voyages Ishmael alludes to,
or the five-long years father
spent his youth on military transport.
No, hard as Hell to fathom that.

When I do
contemplate it,
it's the difference
in the scent of distant
ocean, & smell of air above
earth comes strangely to mind.

The longing there. In the distinction.

So it comes as a surprise here
near the end of the Logbook that
Thoreau steps in as guide back home.
In his posthumous publication, **The Maine Woods,**
he records a trip up to Old Town, meeting the Penobscot

Governor, eighty-nine-year-old, Old John Neptune,
who recalled when moose were much larger than
in Thoreau's time, that in fact, according legend,
down near the Merrimack a whale swam in,
& as the tide went out, stranded, the whale
stood up & walked on land, "Moose was
whale once," said Old John Neptune.

Were I to identify with that
mythological transmogrification
it's again the distinction of the scent
of the air in the distant sea, for whale
& sailor alike, & air above land for moose
& his trek from the Merrimack, which I've trekked
along, & his migration all the way up to the forests of Maine.

I take a deep breath, where both earth & sea air circulate,
give thanks to Thoreau for recording that story,
& guiding me back to Port.

Newest Dream Animal

In the dream last night, as snow fell on the Ninth
day of April like some cascading symphony,
we stood in line, my artistic collaborator
& I, the one who earlier in the week,
in yet another dream showed
me the minor stigmata
on his hands, blood
still flowing
from wounds, we stood
in line with our artwork waiting
for those behind closed doors to open
& take a look at what we'd done. Standing
there in the line with a number of other artists,

we held the long collage, as long as a canoe, & sleek
inside a white covering. Tedious in that way to have
to wait, especially in a dream, where one desires
things to move on rapidly, which they usually
do under our rapid eye movement of sleep,
but no, the curators were busy with what
must be administrative undertakings?

So I took out my sketchbook & drew
a woolly mammoth to accompany the whale
& bull as yet another god-like creature, not a bad
resemblance drawn by the hand of the dream, when
my friend added a number of charcoal marks as ancient,
painted ceiling to house this newest dream animal in a cave,
as if it were the center of a labyrinth, or depth of vast & massive

sea.

Sound at the End of the Road

Get word from one friend he's on the road to Baltimore
at the same juncture I'm crossing the line
into Hiram, Oxford County.

Just here, where the massive granite ledge north
gives way to two bodies of water underneath
bisected by the road.

In my head I'm carrying along that newfound adage
that the goal distracts from attention to
the moment, but I don't forget where I'm going.

My longtime friend is waiting at the end of this trip
for a few parcels & supplies promised him:
deepest red beet soup I ever made;

decent bottle of French *Minervois*;
three loaves of bread
& wedge of blue sheep cheese.

Not a bad haul.
Useful gifts to help celebrate
his birthday the next day.

Bach in the background when he invites me in.
Bach's own birthday when he invites me in
with *Lute Suite in G Minor* playing, perfect

accompaniment to our conversation,

what with various chords broken
into tonal components, in tune

with our own quiet speech
& intervals
of silence.

We know each other well enough
amid the myriad of books
& paintings, sculpture,

computer screens
& keyboards
to gather added meaning

from these intermittent pauses
accompanied as they are by Bach
in the immediate & distant background.

The Unraveling

Blanket like a shroud at three-thirty in the morning
on Friday is returning to pre-life warp & weft
before the weave, prior to primitive loom,
to sheep's clothing, to pasture.

It's cold in the burning night.

Rilke's fear in Brigge's eyes
before Baudelaire's prose walks
on wobbly legs of a Parisian swan
into the Seine.

Thread of the blanket unraveling
a scene twenty-five years old.

Look at us tramp streets of cities looking for mature selves
in young bodies, when young bodies suffice
inside cheap rooms over red wine
or clear alcohol.
Don't look.

The blanket unravels in silence late at night in the burning memory
of nothing regretted,
though lost,
the task of mourning complete in Penelope's unraveling threads
of a past surging toward a future
now.

Quiet the lyric noise.
We forget the length of pain,
of monotony,
of longing.
Write it down.
Flesh should have raging
immediacy enough
to speak for itself.

The Red Thread

Get out there in the cold, where the cold makes one
hunger for safety & comfort
of those less fortunate: that homeless
guy on the side of the road able to sustain
more pain than I ever could, or young woman
with cardboard sign on crossroad island
between east & west traffic,
& even pigeons & crows,
for that matter, so little left to them.

That cold, though winter's
somehow got through & over,
sun's no help yet, nor earth's
axial tilt toward equator.

Cruising up Preble Street toward
the soup kitchen Bill Evans
comes on live in Paris, 1979
Quiet Now. Tempted
not to say another word,
I can't help, but moan
a bit of nothing other
than compassion for
contemporaries
I see all around me,
while America goes on worshiping
celebrity, rewarding mediocrity,
perpetuating inherited
wealth.

Once home, the red thread sewn into black corduroy
keeping jacket cuffs from fraying,
faintly emerges above keyboard
to add a line here commenting
on my own precarious
& dire straits.

Cardboard Put to Good Use

This thin piece of cardboard once held
a pad of hotel notepaper,
now dispersed
in notes & jottings,
but cardboard put to good use
as bookmark now far away
from Aalborg, Bremen,
Cambridge, Denver,
Elk City, Oklahoma?
I don't know.

Notes & jottings
scattered here & there,
snowflakes
in the archive?

Meanwhile, cardboard
put to good use
holds my place
open
to Rome,
where James Wright
will, once again, empathize
with both martyrs
& hungry
lions.

Five for the Homeless

I. Twenty Lines for the Homeless

On the seventh of the first month of the year
you can hear the cold in all its silence
banging on the walls, frigid, fractal,
anesthetizing, indifferently brutal.
She had a deep furrowed brow,
eyes closed, saying prayers
for the homeless, under
extra layers, almost
in tears sensing
the irony.

The sound of the cold on the seventh day
of the first month of the year keeps one
awake in trepidation. Some shelters
have no beds. Nothing, but bare
floors. Occupants there can't
hear the silence of the cold,
but rather the murmur
of each others'
struggling
breath.

II. This Sky's Beauty

The Arctic Express zooming in, not from the Northwest,
but due North, carries new light via its grey frontal
clouds vying with sunrise. Verging on a mixture
of purple & green perhaps only Monet could
manufacture. Opposite the surface content
of water lilies, this sky's beauty rests
solely in the realm of cruelty.

III. Rich City, Wrong Song

Even the new light against neighbors'
third-story windows echo sounds
of the brutal cold & homeless.
Snow remains in every
crotch of tree. Ice
seals each road
& sidewalk.

At the Soup Kitchen it hurts to stand
in line before the place even opens.
Flesh shivering, teeth chattering.
To eavesdrop on those voices
is to listen to another version
of the silence of the cold.
Rich city, wrong song.

IV. Except, Remember?

These silences of the cold, murmurs
of the homeless remind me that
I lost a job once, finding
myself out on the street
on Thanksgiving Day.

Desolate city streets empty.
Except. Except, remember
the guy with jaw long
deformed checking
the phone booth
for change?

Gave both him & a distraught
woman, old, alone, obviously
homeless what money I had
(2 *finnifs*) before returning
to my own one-room pad,
grateful, blessed by grace
of two strangers?

V. Murmur of Breath

We're told it'll be eight below overnight
with added, indifferent, meteorological
wind-chill calculations tossed in
like invisible charitable felt
blankets slung around
homeless shoulders.

For now, however, Boccherini's *Quintetto*
con due viole in do floating over waves
from Venice Classic Radio is in stark
contrast to the sound of the cold
heard for hours with murmur
of the breath of homeless.

Here at Home with Steamer Trunks Once Belonged to
Mr. & Mrs. Albert Kreglinger

Walking down along my own beloved Portland waterfront,
just as Gloucester was for years, & Salem's Derby Wharf off
Orange Street (four roads over from Hawthorne's birthplace),
where Pattie & Bobby Leonard lived & hosted a dinner party
the night before we headed cross-country down to Mexico as
far as Veracruz, it's this Logbook's on my mind, anonymous
tanker in the shimmering distance, Queequeg's tattoos, & even
my own tattoos as passport to the world.

What with Brad headed to Portugal tomorrow, David to Venice,
I'm here at home with new steamer trunks once belonged to
Mr. & Mrs. Albert Kreglinger of 9 Grand Place, Antwerp, Coltrane
blowing hard on Miles' *Teo* to help me sail through this navigational
whirlwind of places I've been, shoved prow-first against destinations
I long to go, no, I'll gladly stay at home with her, & travel via imagination,
memory, & Coltrane's southwest wind today on tenor sax helping me sail
clear across the Atlantic to Howth Head in Dublin, where Yeats attempted
to romance Maud Gonne to little avail on across to Calais that first day
in France off the Dover ferry, where mates & I drank Stella Artois all day
& night, sleeping in a railroad boxcar till gendarmes rousted us up & out
on down to the first day in Nice, where the dumb Dutch guy preached
one should kill rare animals, then they'd be rarer, & gendarmes took
my passport, tossed me in the paddy wagon with German & Dutch
hippies. Can't get enough of Coltrane on *Teo* today so place track 5
on repeat, where this walk along Portland waterfront brings into view

this bare-chested dude coming toward me next

to Portland Yacht Services flaunting his myriad of tattoos

in the most prideful manner possible, my aversion to such obvious

hubris I have to look away calling on his opposite in Queequeg & how

Melville details his hieroglyphics as portrayal by the shaman of Kokovoko,

shaman of Kokovoko, Kokovoko shaman Coltrane on *Teo*,

as theory of the workings of heaven & earth, a tract

on the skin in one volume, an open book, the ink

of those tattoos yet unable to hide the soul,

or an honest heart.

Port-of-Call

So yesterday's anonymous tanker rises up past the gantry
carrying the offload of oil blocked the name of the ship,
Suez Fuzeyya, which of course, in its far-reaching
intimation reminds one of Baudelaire waxing
nostalgic in his prose poem, *Sea-Ports*,
in **Paris Spleen**, linking me to
the discrepancy between
desire to travel & lack
of wherewithal to
do so.

Baudelaire says a seaport is the perfect venue for a Soul
run out of energy to go beyond the confines of, say, his own
Honfleur, which may or not be him, but calls it an aristocratic
perspective to have lost all curiosity & desire to go any further,
while taking vicarious pleasure in those who arrive & depart, those
who still desire to voyage, or get rich.

I might desire to voyage, always have, always will, even if the destination
is Death itself.

But the aversion to hubris referred to yesterday is the same
aversion to those who desire too much money, or for the most part,
those I've met who already possess just that, which seems to go hand-
in-hand with the great Greek dramatists' notion of excessive pride.

No, give me St. Francis of Paola, who founded the order of Minims.
Comparable to Kerouac's *Bhikkhu*, Minims were founded on the idea
of *the least of the faithful* with humility as their forte toward a Good Life.

Here I am, simply jotting down impressions
of a walking/sailing life, while heading toward yet
another port-of-call: the Soul of my very Self, if that's the case.

Newly-Invented Chord

Put it this way with another brutal week
of winter left till Spring: Times one
ought to open the lid of the black
lacquered piano, & for sound
accompaniment, instead
of playing keys
connected to
hammers
covered
in felt
cloth
from
a decent
height hold
a large spike in hand
above inside steel strings,
& after deciding which one
wants to enact, cacophony or
music, as the case may be, drop it
free-fall from a standing position stepping
on the right-side sustain pedal at the same Time,
allowing the newly-invented chord to resonate out
into the universe carrying one's rage or praise till Spring.

Whose Open Mouth Doubles as Sharp Arc of Bird's Wing

Drawn down there,
just as I'm drawn inside
here to hear what language
wells up, intuitively, magnetically,
one could say toward that North, suddenly
the male osprey flies overhead with good-sized
twig in his beak dangling building material for nest
now come into view through binoculars in his landing.

It's a sign. Confluence of dwelling. Watch him insert
branch instinctively reinforcing the wall, all
the while I'm thinking he'd like to build
a roof, if he could, knowing it's
a projection on my part,
on one hand calling
on Frank Speck in
Penobscot Man
documenting
early shelter
recounted
then only

from memory,
either conical birch-
bark wigwams, or more
permanent round houses,
or even makeshift lean-tos
made of evergreen boughs by
hunters on the move, & confirmed

by Jacques Cartier as far back as 1534.

Female osprey pops her head up, then lone
chick a bit wobbly woken by the master builder,
while up from my own cave of being comes the ancient
image I once saw drawn out of stone, sculpturally: horse
head whose open mouth doubles as sharp arc of bird's wing
equal to this raptor flying off again, either to hunt, or to gather.

Animated Landscape

On the shore of the Kennebec River, not far
from the village of Solon, Maine, fair distance
from Athens, further from Harmony,
petroglyphs show evidence

of shamanistic power,
including birds & phalloi,
vulvas & snakes, canoes & unknown
symbols, all of which archaeologist,

Dean Snow, interprets as personal
charisma & sexual potency
associated with northern
sagamores.

However, the very act of creating these glyphs
seems to reveal a desire to share
magical energy derived
from art.

Wigwams are pictured
together as the initial imagery,
while moon comes down to join
birds, dogs, & females.

Away from the village, along the river, men row
both canoe & wiki-up, dog perched atop roof.
Bands track wolves. One man's hand
is larger than his head.

The final image of river transport offers a sense of distance
spanning the entire interior:
an early animated
landscape.

With Me Here in Portland

Used **Pleistocene Man** as bookmark
to mark the page in Max Raphael, where
he states: *The Paleolithics constantly felt their*
lives in danger & this feeling contributed to their
sense of empirical existence to the level of Being, then
leaps in the very next sentence to Van Eyck & Masaccio
as examples of men so sure of the ground underneath them
that they painted with similar grace comparable to Altamira.

These letters by Olson written in 1965
to Jack Clarke, with whom I had the privilege
of playing poker & talking poetry late into the night
a number of times, get right at Jung on Alchemy, & Mellart
on Asia, Osborne the Pleistocene's earliest human experiences.

All this outside under a wild apple in full bloom <u>after </u>reading
the long letter from Bill Heyen & his poem showing a Swedish friend
at the gravestone of EZRA POUND. All this, while sitting at a picnic table
on Memorial Day Weekend knowing that men hunted on this very ground when
the glaciers failed to cover this rocky cliff, materiel & cunning visible in the geography
covered over by encroachment of previous three centuries.

Even these hillside birches got their skin/bark color from the glacier in the distance,
which fled ten thousand years ago cutting its way through Casco Bay Islands.
I always imagine their ancestors, the trees, waving goodbye to the ice,
but not necessarily the cold. It's not long today before Raphael gets
to the same root Olson got to in March of 1953: the artist's
<u>compulsion</u>, his will, & this <u>compulsion</u>, in opposition,
sees through the controlling aspects of the ruling

class ~~before this class has the strength to thwart~~

It's almost as if both writers were still alive,
the Olson bookmark carrying on a conversation
with the Raphael text riding crosstown to this spot
on the edge of the cliff, the latter's Franco-Cantabrian
sources intersecting with the former's Paleo-American,
similar to the way 43 degrees in latitude match perfectly
across the Atlantic linking Castillo & Altamira with me here
in Portland.

When Senses Reach Intoxicated Height

Sea went out so far we wondered
in our sensual blur if it might not return.
Color of lone sail on horizon, maroon.
Minor waves hypnotized us into trance.
She said she caught sight of endlessness.

So many hues of blue we reimagined
Ezra Pound at Sirmio in between Brescia
& Verona, where L'ago di Garda turned
sapphire cobalt cyanine three shades of azure
& its waves *unstill of eternal change.*

No, no Sirmio, here yet our geography is
not impoverished, when senses reach an
intoxicated height, where air alone is
magic, silence music, touch between
us dispelling all dread.

Kept at Bay by Some Reason, or Another

Walked out there, where night was,
under a late blue sky,
that is, I couldn't
figure out why
darkness was in front of me,
light above, but took it, as it was, to heart.

Walked looking upward, wondering
why there were no stars in the sky, to the point
where I could have stumbled down,
staring up, done in by walkway
cracks, or curb divides.
The way sustained me, anciently.

I trudged on with Goya on my mind,
wondering how often he depicted stars,
rather than moon or clouds above a convocation
of true-believing
heathens.

Then this incredible turnaround: in the meantime,
between entering the corner store
for a bottle *Casa Solar Tempranillo*,
& heading home in the same darkness traversed at eye-level
on the way there, darkness flew up
to call stars down.

In the simplest temporal interval, everything changed.
Goya's haunting demons

from one of the *Caprichos,*
In the morning, we shall go, threatened to intervene,
& I welcomed their company into my loneliness.
But they stayed away, kept at bay
by some reason, or another.

In a matter of minutes, during the Time it took
to decide which wine was cheapest,
& good, at the same Time,
sky blackened.

Stars pierced the immense blackness.
Constellations stood in
for Timelessness.

Ancient, Ancestral Tongue

It's just that.
Once one's on the path,
the way opens up,
as if right there before
& coming toward one, say,
an opportune collision
today of shell midden
& gleaning heads
& racks of four
broiled mackerel
cooked days ago.

Ate, as I gleaned them, while inherited
ancient, ancestral tongue searched,
analyzed, divided, rejected,
protecting the throat
with quite a bit
of millennial
finesse
in tandem
with teeth & jaw,
fingers better equipped
than bear's paw at getting
to cheek meat, brain fat, even
gelatinous tongue of the fish itself.

At the same time I find Guy Davenport reporting
that the midden from which a hen digs a letter
up from Boston in **Finnegan's Wake:**

is Joyce's symbol for the deep forgotten past,
a past recorded sensitively & beautifully
in cave walls, on bone, in sculpture,
on flint tools, rings of megaliths,
and mounds of earth depicting
running horses, ithyphallic
giants, and serpents.

Guy once wrote
me that he'd spoken
one Sunday morning on
the phone to Hallam Movius,
his number given by Alexander Marshack.

Coincidence, collision
one could say, or the event
Olson claimed can only occur
when one's Self & Eternity collide,
is that the call to Movius was while writing
this very essay, *Prehistoric Eyes.*

Here, Marshack turns the previous supposition of the mackerel etched
on bone with mouth closed to that of salmon, mouth open, & seal
supposedly following it upriver now, a flower, or tree,
coinciding with Olson's belief in the historical
importance of weeds & crops to the extent
that he says, *where man began is where*
you begin…: We begin with what
is under foot.

Drama of My Own & the World's Making

Just two days into summer,
sun & stones met for what seemed
at first mere discourse, but soon doves
& mockingbirds chimed in making it a chorus.
Theriomorphic lines jumped out, as if they were
the makeshift first stage for goat dance & earliest Greek
satyr play.

Finches flocked around me
as the audience
of one.

I, too, then jumped down a ledge
& leapt across an abyss deep
enough to add a certain beat,
a drum.

Another drumbeat of two boots against
ancient stones leading to all this fresh
edible seaweed shore's edge, where
the drama of my own & the world's
making came to an end, but not
forgotten.

Named by Basque Fishermen

Archaeologists see the influx
of Susquehanna Broad Points north
to the middle of the Maine Maritime
during the Terminal Archaic Period
as evidence of small groups coexisting.

However, Dean Snow,
in his **Archaeology of New England**,
has to use evidence found in Watertown, Mass
in order to address ceremonial mortuary practices,
where the people buried: cremated bone; burnt
& broken artifacts; & red ochre; usually
placed in a pit of black, greasy soil
that resembles rich midden
soil, perhaps redeposited
cremation residue.

It's his map,
which shows the coast
not covered by glacial ice
at least as far back as 16 thousand years ago,
which is also of interest: Bull Brook, Ipswich,
Cape Ann, Portland, & the entire rocky coast of Maine
to Nova Scotia, & as Olson knew, to Port au Choix,
Newfoundland, named by Basque fishermen,
no less, *the little port*, & inhabited
by Beothuk, or Red Paint People.

One's reminded here of the poet's belief

that the cave at Castillo

lines up in almost

exact latitude

with Cape Ann,

& there are his Basques gliding

sidewise across the Atlantic, descendants

of Cro-Magnon, as Russell Martin conjectures

in **Picasso's War.**

Picasso's Own, End of the Road

Found it there sifting through old postcards
from travelers through every state in America.
Here's Picasso's own, *End of the Road*, oil wash
& crayon on paper, drawn in 1898 at only seventeen,
the year he caught scarlet fever. The procession of old
& young streams long before us & imagined behind
with crutches & canes, horse & wagon, the woman
in the foreground cradling an emaciated child
with bandaged head, bodies becoming black
shadows as they approach the winged angel
of Death.

As if Placed in Celestial Good Graces

Up & out early for as much light
as possible - summer this far north starts late,
then ushers fall & winter in too soon.

Two trees, again, adding to the vision.
Flowers of concentrated molecular color
in catalpa at one end of the street & chestnut

at the other. Majestic, tall, with sturdy trunks,
scattering white purple & yellow petals
& pistils onto black pavement.

Joy, as a kid I envisioned grace falling
from heaven to earth, more gold
back then than yellow & white.

Carried this extra light along to city's center,
joining office workers strolling with a quick
bite away from desks, savoring noon.

Back home Beethoven coming over waves from Venice Radio
with Isaac Stern, violin - Leonard Rose, cello - Eugene Istomin,
piano on his *Erzherzog-Trio*, which premiered three hundred & one

years ago, one of the composer's final performances before
deafness set in. Talk & silence dovetailed between us
during the rest of the evening, until after nine

I found the day wasn't finished & called her
to witness any light left in the Western sky.
As if placed in celestial good graces Venus
shimmered voluptuously low on the horizon,
while Jupiter sidled up close behind her.
We two held on to each other as well.

Could be I'd absorbed enough warm light
inside me in this one day to last long
past chill & darkness of the grave.

The World Takes a Different Tact

The world spent a great deal of Time shaking
sense into me.
Thankful for those irruptions, quakes, thunderbolts,
wasp stings, & praise
gut-wrenching punches,
Proustian slaps across the face,
or missteps
on Boston cobbles.

But now, the world takes a different tact.
Must figure I've paid some dues,
in full.

Sets up situations
where stasis has a message,
where calm waters want undercurrents
understood in juxtaposition
to clarity
of an endless
sky above.

Just as difficult to register
the scale of *this* world's impact
on the radial focal point within oneself.

Not that one prefers the tempest.

I've touched down,
whirlwind & stillness
blessed.

To Illuminate the Night for an Instant

Our dream realm & the Prehistoric, where last night
the great Black Bull metamorphosed right before
my unconscious eye into the Black Cave Bear.
Hide into fur, which three brave men petted
to keep the massive animal calm. Then,
just before waking a circular mandala/
labyrinth of finely woven web, where
the spider took the Minotaur's place
in the center. In *The Labyrinth*
Georges Bataille claims
THE UNIVERSAL resembles
the Bull with its nonchalance of animality
& secret paleness of Death, watched over by
a skeletal torero. Bataille guffaws a laugh of Joy
before what he sees as the nudity of Nothingness
& Death. Little Feminine spider residing in the center
of the delicate web of a perfect mandala/labyrinth must have
had a smile on her face in order *to illuminate the night for an instant.*

Next to Each Other, Silent

It's better to imagine death
than think & talk about the inevitable
pain & agony ahead of it.

I saw us in the dream next
to each other, silent,
underground.

Not so much different
than last night, or
the night before.

AFTERWORD: There's Still Time

It's almost cruel now that we, too, will refer to "the last century," when Olson found himself hammering away at the origin of "character" as that which marks, makes sharp, engraves, insisting on a vertical poetics that digs, unearths. Why in the last century I was so enamored of those ancient stone tools, especially the tooth-sharp burin first used to separate fur & skin from meat of the animal taken down by shaft or arrow, & later incising lines inside the cave. Character become letter emblazoned into language into internal traits of tribe & individuality. Writing is a forceful act, physical, demanding, delving, ruthless, oracular. Unless it's merely business, politics, or law. Art drives down. Depths equal to marrow, sex, death; reemerging breathing light. Psychologists may see character as fixed, inexorable, but writers & artists view it as changeable, inscribable. There's still Time.

Robert Gibbons is the author of nine books of poetry, numerous chapbooks, and a unique study of the affinities in approaches to art in language by Charles Olson and that of Clyfford Still in paint: **Olson/Still: Crossroad.** In 2006 he was awarded a John Anson Kittredge Fund grant to travel and read his work at the Poetry & Politics Conference at the University of Stirling, Scotland. There, he met Ben Bollig, now at Oxford, who recorded the meeting online writing that, "he is the most passionate advocate of poetry I have met." National Book Award Finalist, William Heyen, calls Gibbons "one of the great writers of our time." In 2013, after publishing his *Trilogy* of prose poems, **This Time, Traveling Companion,** and **To Know Others, Various & Free,** the poet was invited to give the Creative Keynote address, titled *Kerouac & the Ecstatic Act of Writing,* at the 2nd annual European Beat Studies Conference held at Aalborg University, Denmark. For the past 12 years he's lived and worked in Portland, Maine. Former chairman of PEN New England, Richard Hoffman, wrote, "Gibbons is in the process of sacralizing Portland, lodging it in the imagination of readers, as Williams did for Paterson, Cafavy for Alexandria, Joyce for Dublin."

But there is also new pleasure to found here: Gibbons has embraced a free verse style that allows him to use the page in new ways that his adherence to the prose poem did not. Here we see slabs of text move across the pages as slow tectonic plates, or rapid mud slides down a mountainside. We see hills and valleys and streams of text flow up and down the pages as well, or are they banners waving in the strong winds of the poetic breath?

As always, Gibbons acknowledges generously his poetic debts. Olson looms large, as do – more subtly – Ginsberg and Whitman. My favorite poem in this collection is the meditation on decay and potential rejuvenation titled "Think of Detroit". To me this poem is the "Wichita Vortex Sutra" of the second decade of the 21st century – written 50 years after Ginsberg spoke his stream of consciousness poem into a tape recorder, breathing forth his vision of the American landscape of the Vietnam War era. Gibbons' poem also speaks of the economy and the destruction of lives in the wake of capitalism's cruel logic. But using the twin figures of Frida Kahlo and Diego Rivera it also offers a vortex of positive, creative energy, unifying the apparently distant places of the Mexican border and the bleak industrial north – and the people who dwell in those animated landscapes. —**Bent Sørensen**

Made in the USA
Middletown, DE
29 August 2016